WHERE IS MY HOME?

by Robin Nelson

Lerner Publications Company · Minneapolis

I live in a house.

This house is my **home.**

My home is where I live
with my family.

My home is on a street
with other homes.

My street is in
a **neighborhood.**

My neighborhood
is in a **town.**

Some families live in
homes in a **city.**

Some families live in
homes in the **country.**

Families live all
around the world.

There are different kinds of
homes all around the world.

There are big homes.

There are small homes.

There are old homes.

There are new homes.

Where is my home?

My home is in my town,
where I live with my family.

What do you see in this neighborhood?

What do you see in your neighborhood?

Home Facts

 Apartments are homes in large buildings that contain many individual homes all together.

 Some people live on a boat. This kind of home is called a houseboat.

 The largest home in the world is a palace owned by the Sultan of Brunei in Asia. It cost $422 million to build. It has 1,788 rooms, 257 toilets, and an underground garage.

A trailer is a small house on wheels.

The U.S. president's home, the White House, is in Washington, D.C. It has 6 floors, 132 rooms, 32 bathrooms, 147 windows, 412 doors, 28 fireplaces, 12 chimneys, 3 elevators, and 7 staircases. It also has a tennis court, jogging track, swimming pool, movie theater, billiard room, and bowling lane.

Glossary

 city – a place where many people live and work. A city is a large town.

 country – an area away from a city where few people live

 home – a place where people live

 neighborhood – the homes and people who live around you

 town – a place where people live and work. A town is smaller than a city.

Index

The photographs in this book are reproduced through the courtesy of: © Wolfgang Kaehler, front cover, pp. 3, 5, 7, 8, 10, 11, 12, 13, 14, 22 (top, middle, and bottom); © Bud Titlow/Visuals Unlimited, p. 2; © Jeff Greenberg/Visuals Unlimited, pp. 4, 16; © Mark E. Gibson/Visuals Unlimited, pp. 6, 22 (second from bottom); © Inga Spence/Visuals Unlimited, pp. 9, 22 (second from top); © Stephen Graham Photography, p. 15; © Martin Rogers/Stone, p. 17.

Lerner Publications Company
A division of Lerner Publishing Group
241 First Avenue North
Minneapolis, MN 55401 U.S.A.

Website address: www.lernerbooks.com

Library of Congress Cataloging-in-Publication Data

Nelson, Robin, 1971–
    Where is my home? / by Robin Nelson.
        p.   cm. — (First step nonfiction)
    Includes index.
    ISBN: 0–8225–0189–9 (lib. bdg. : alk. paper)
    1. Dwellings—Juvenile literature. 2. Family life—Juvenile literature. [1. Dwellings.]
I. Title. II. Series.
GT170.N45 2002
392.3'6—dc21   2001000963

Manufactured in the United States of America
1 2 3 4 5 6 – AM – 07 06 05 04 03 02